SUNDAY
MORNING
LIVE

Willow Creek Resources is a publishing partnership between Zondervan Publishing House and the Willow Creek Association. Willow Creek Resources will include drama sketches, small group curricula, training material, videos, and many other specialized ministry resources.

Willow Creek Association is an international network of churches ministering to the unchurched. Founded in 1992, the Willow Creek Association serves churches through conferences, seminars, regional roundtables, consulting, and ministry resource materials. The mission of the Association is to assist churches in reestablishing the priority and practice of reaching lost people for Christ through church ministries targeted to seekers.

For conference and seminar information please write to:

Willow Creek Association
P.O. Box 3188
Barrington, Illinois 60011-3188

SUNDAY MORNING LIVE

VOLUME 1

A Collection of Drama Sketches
from Willow Creek Community Church

Edited by Steve Pederson

ZondervanPublishingHouse
Grand Rapids, Michigan
A Division of HarperCollins*Publishers*

WILLOW
CREEK
RESOURCES

Sunday Morning Live
Copyright © 1992 by Willow Creek Community Church
All rights reserved

Requests for information should be addressed to:
Zondervan Publishing House
Grand Rapids, Michigan 49530

Library of Congress Cataloging-in-Publication Data

Sunday morning live : a collection of drama sketches from Willow Creek Community
   Church / edited by Steve Pederson.
      p.   cm.
    Summary: A collection of contemporary drama sketches which raise Biblical
questions.
    ISBN 0-310-59221-6
    1. Christian drama, American. (1. Christian life—Drama. 2. Plays.) I. Pederson,
Steve. II. Willow Creek Community Church (South Barrington, Ill.)
    PS627.R4S8   1992   92-26029
    812'.54080382–dc20   CIP
                                                    AC

Edited by Lori J. Walburg
Cover design by Cheryl Van Andel

Printed in the United States of America

   93 94 95 96 / ❖   / 10 9 8 7 6 5 4 3

To Nancy Beach,

*director of creative arts programming
at Willow Creek Community Church.
Nancy exemplifies godly leadership
and has consistently been our best cheerleader.
Her vision and commitment to excellence
has strongly influenced the development
of drama at Willow Creek.*

Contents

About the Contributors

Donna Hinkle Lagerquist has been a part of the Willow Creek drama team for eleven years and a writer for five. Her sketch *Stolen Jesus* is being adapted into a Canadian Television Christmas special. She and her husband, Paul, are expecting their first child. They live in Cary, Illinois.

Debra Poling has a degree in Language Arts Education from the University of Wisconsin, Milwaukee. She has been a contributor to the drama team for ten years. With Sharon Sherbondy, she is the author of *Super Sketches,* a drama collection for high school students. Debra and Judson have two children and live in Algonquin, Illinois.

Judson Poling was drama director at Willow Creek for five years. He now serves on Willow Creek's staff in the area of small groups leadership training. Judson is also co-author of the *Walking With God Series,* Willow Creek's small groups curriculum. Judson holds a Master of Divinity degree from Trinity Evangelical Divinity School.

Sharon Sherbondy has been a member of the drama team for fourteen years and a writer for eight. Her drama ministry has taken her throughout the United States and abroad. She is the co-author of *Super Sketches,* a finalist for the Gold Medallion Book Award. She home schools her two children and lives with her husband, Steve, in Elgin, Illinois.

Introduction

In 1975, Willow Creek Community Church began in a rented movie theater in suburban Chicago. Founded with the expressed purpose of reaching the nonchurched, today Willow Creek attracts upwards of 15,000 people to its weekend "seeker services."

Since the beginning, drama has been an integral part of Willow Creek's outreach. Different from traditional church drama, these sketches are short, six- to eight-minute, contemporary vignettes, rooted in real-life experience. Today many churches all over the country, both large and small, are using these sketches as a powerful part of their ministry.

The Message "Set Up"

These sketches are not intended to stand on their own. Rather, they are used to create interest in an issue by grabbing the attention of the audience and getting them to identify with the characters. Also, the sketches do not provide easy answers, but instead raise questions, which the pastor then seeks to answer in the message. Much of the material in this volume may seem "secular," in that there is no specific "Christian" content in the sketch itself. However, when performed in connection with a biblically based message that addresses the same question or problem, the sketch takes on spiritual significance.

This separation of drama and message is a major difference between Willow Creek's approach to drama and that traditionally taken by many churches. While difficult for some people to accept, such a separation is supported by dramatic tradition throughout history. Dorothy Sayers, Christian playwright and novelist, summed it up well: "Playwrights are not evangelists." A dictum frequently repeated to aspiring playwrights is "if you have a message, send it to Western Union." At Willow Creek we try not to abuse drama as an art form by manipulating it to preach a message. Simply put, the sketches clarify the "bad news" so the pastor can bring the "good news."

The Audience "Set Up"

A sketch cannot "set up" a message if viewers do not, in some way, see themselves mirrored in the action. Drama works because people experience vicariously what characters act out on stage. We want to engage not only the minds, but also the emotions of our audience. And drama, which results in high identification, appeals to people's hearts as well as their heads.

At Willow Creek we use contemporary "slice of life" drama, rather than enacted biblical stories, because people more readily identify with characters who act and talk like they do and who confront the same daily issues. This approach helps us earn the right to be heard, because our seekers realize that the church is in touch with the real world, where real people live, work, and struggle.

For example, consider the couple in the sketch *An Hour On Wednesday*. While their problem is exaggerated, it is not unlike what many of us face in our own attempts to juggle the competing demands of work and family. We hope that many people will see themselves, to some degree, reflected in these characters. The appropriate message following this sketch "set up" could point out that the problems we face in our fast-paced lifestyle are often the result of a value system gone awry because we live without a spiritual foundation.

We've discovered that the degree of audience identification directly parallels what we call the "reality factor." Drama earns credibility with an audience when it is honest and truthful in how it handles material. If drama comes off simplistic and naïve, or presents clichéd, easy answers, it will not produce the desired result. The gulf between the couple in *An Hour on Wednesday* can't be bridged with some simple formula. Even a more broadly satirical sketch, such as *Is "Nothing" Sacred?* needs to be based in a recognizable reality in order to work.

The sketch *I Don't Want to Fight You Anymore* depicts a woman caught in a spiritual quandary. She would like to give complete control of her life over to God, but her emotions are making it difficult for her. She comes to the painful realization that the poor relationship she had with her earthly father makes it very difficult for her to trust her heavenly Father. The "reality factor" comes in the opening and closing lines of the monologue when the woman says to God, "Life was so much simpler before I met you." Some people may cringe at the thought of a character saying this in church, because it seems to contradict what the church is trying to teach. But since it realistically affirms what many people feel, the audience will identify strongly with it. This sketch, followed by a carefully crafted message, could show the audience that while submission to the Lordship of Christ is difficult, it is also worth the struggle.

If drama for seekers is to be effective in the church, we must be passionately committed to being real, warts and all. We must avoid easy answers, because they ultimately don't help, even if they sound good. Seekers and believers alike want truth, not a sugar-coated, sanitized version of reality.

In his book *Open Windows*, in a chapter entitled "Pitfalls of Christian Writing," Philip Yancey laments:

> Sometimes when I read Christian books, especially in the fields of fiction and biography, I have a suspicion that characters have been strangely lobotomized. . . . Just as a lobotomy flattens out emotional peaks and valleys, Christian writers can tend to safely reduce life's tensions and strains to a more acceptable level. . . . A perverse fear of overstatement keeps us confined to that flatland realm of "safe" emotions and tensions—a fear that seems incredible in light of the biblical model.

The cause of Christ would be well served if the church would listen to Yancey. For it is truth-telling (which isn't very safe) that not only gives ministry integrity, but also opens up seekers to the possibility of transformation through the power of the Gospel.

Getting Started

The sketch format is a fairly easy way for any church, regardless of size, to begin using drama. A little time, a few simple props, a couple of actors (in some cases just one), and a director are all the necessary elements.

Because sketches are short, the time demand for rehearsals is not excessive. Typically, we spend about four to five hours rehearsing each one. If you are working with relatively inexperienced people, however, it would probably be wise to plan more time. Our four hours is divided into two rehearsals. The actors pick up their scripts one week before the performance. Our first rehearsal is early in the week, during which time we discuss the characters and work out the basic movement (blocking). Because we have only two rehearsals, we ask the actors to memorize the script prior to this rehearsal, with the goal of being off the script by the end of the two-hour session.

For the second rehearsal—in our case, before it is performed for the first service—we rehearse one and a half hours, working on stage with the hand props and furniture we'll be using. During this time we polish the movement, work on character consistency, pacing, and the rise and fall of the action. If movement doesn't look natural because an actor is having a hard time making it look motivated, we change it. After we're off the stage, we run lines or work problem areas of blocking for an additional half to full hour. We also try to relax and enjoy each other's company before the service begins.

For props, we use only that which is absolutely necessary. In other words, we don't use furniture to establish setting, but only if it fulfills a necessary function in the sketch. If, for example, a phone is needed, we would use an end table to set it on. But if nothing needs to sit on the end table, why use one? Typically we do not use door or window units. If a window is called for, as in *Tired When Needed,* we mime it. However, rather than mime the opening and closing of an imaginary door, which gets cumbersome, the actors simply enter a room, a convention which an audience seems to accept.

Although it doesn't happen often, sometimes a scenic element greatly enhances a sketch. For example, *Tired When Needed* requires a door because some of the conversation occurs between two characters on opposite sides of a motel room door. Staging this with only an imagined door would probably look strange. Furthermore, a real door helps establish the idea that Mr. Watkins is trying to escape to a safe, undemanding place. He wants to "close out" the world, and an actual door helps to underscore this point.

A simple rule of thumb for the use of props and scenic pieces is to use only what is necessary, keeping them simple and relying on the audience's imagination to fill in the details. Not only is this an easier route, but—unless you have a professional set designer—it is also the most effective. Furthermore, since props usually need to be set in place before a sketch and removed afterwards, the simpler you can keep it, the better.

While the technical elements necessary to produce a good sketch are fairly basic, assembling the right actors and someone to "lead the charge" might prove more challenging. Talent in drama, unlike the other arts, is somewhat difficult to assess quickly. If someone cannot sing a song or play an instrument, it is readily evident, but acting talent is more difficult to define. To further complicate the matter, drama seems to attract people who have an affinity for the arts but who lack specific talent or training. Someone reasons, "I can't sing, or play the piano, but I think I can act." Indeed, maybe this person has acting ability, but too often such people are drawn to drama because it appears relatively "easy," at least compared to the other arts. But doing drama well is more difficult than it appears. Unfortunately, many well-intentioned people, because they know little about the craft of drama, have not helped further the cause of drama in the church. God is not served when drama is done poorly.

Therefore, before getting serious about drama, even short sketches, the church must find a competent drama director. This individual needs to have adequate people skills, the ability to assess acting talent, and an understanding of the basics of stage direction. If someone possesses great drama instincts, though lacks formal training, it would be a wise investment for a church to enroll this person in some courses in acting and directing at a local college. A good course in directing can provide many of the basic principles necessary for staging drama effectively.

Having formally trained actors is an advantage, but most churches do not have this luxury—all the more reason to have someone with skill and training leading the team. Over time, talented lay people with good dramatic instincts can develop into strong performers, even if they have no previous drama experience, but their growth will be severely limited if their directors do not have sufficient training.

And finally, a word of encouragement. Once a person has understood some basic principles of theatre—as simple as this sounds—that person learns to do drama by *doing* drama. Even the most inexperienced actors and directors can improve, as long as they are willing to learn from their mistakes.

Throughout our many years of doing drama at Willow Creek, we have made numerous mistakes. We still do. In the earlier years, for example, too many of our scripts were "preachy," and therefore stilted and manipulated. Today, periodically, we do a script that we think will work, but it ends up falling flat, due to a lack of conflict, identification, humor, or any number of factors. Sometimes it is particularly frustrating because it's difficult to figure out exactly why a script appeared not to "go over." Such is the business of doing original drama. But as long as we try to learn from each experience, over time we improve the quality and increase our understanding of the craft of drama.

It is our hope that the "tested" resources in *Sunday Morning Live Volume 1,* and others in volumes to follow, will provide you with at least one of the necessary elements for doing drama—the script.

Based on our experience at Wil- low Creek, these sketches have worked well. We pray they will work well for you, too.

Steve Pederson
Drama Director
Willow Creek
   Community Church

An Hour on Wednesday

Chris and Laura are a couple living in the fast track. Their highly scheduled existence leaves them little time for each other. When Laura reveals she is pregnant, Chris's machinelike response is "February is bad," and Laura is hurt by his insensitivity. While much of the sketch is comic, it moves toward a poignant ending.

SUGGESTED TOPICS: marriage, damaging effects of a fast-paced lifestyle, workaholism

CHARACTERS:

> **Chris**   a high-powered business executive
> **Laura**   his wife, and an executive in her own right

PROPS: Kitchen table set with breakfast dishes, two chairs, coffee pot, sugar and cream set, two muffins, briefcase, Daytimer, microwave, laptop computer, and cordless telephone

An Hour on Wednesday

Sharon Sherbondy

Setting: *Kitchen of Chris and Laura.*

Chris: *(sitting at table, talking on telephone, typing on laptop computer)* All right, so we're scheduled for next Wednesday, 11:00. Now, I'll need the most recent report, showing those updated figures. Right.

Laura: *(rushes in, chipper, putting on her earring)* Morning. *(somewhat discouraged that he's preoccupied)*

Chris: I'll tell you what, let's just make it for lunch. *(Laura pours herself a cup of coffee.)* We're going to be meeting through the noon hour anyways. Yes, check with them to see if they're available.

Laura: *(looks for the cream for her coffee)* Chris, have you seen the cream? *(As she's saying that, he's poured the last drop into his coffee, paying no attention to her. She sees him do it. Looks frustrated. Switches cups with him.)*

Chris: Hey!

Laura: *(lightly)* Thank you.

Chris: I'm sorry. I had an interruption. What were you saying? Right. We'll do it. Good idea. Yeah, I should be there in about forty-five minutes. Okay. *(Hangs up.*

Laura has been heating a muffin in the microwave. She takes it out, puts it on the table in front of her place. Chris takes it.) Thank you.

Laura: *(puts another muffin in the microwave)* Listen, stock's down.

Chris: *(almost chokes)* Down? The market isn't even open yet.

Laura: Check the stock in the refrigerator. We're out of everything.

Chris: Laura, I'd appreciate it if you wouldn't use the term "stock" so loosely. It can be very life-threatening.

Laura: Sorry. I believe it's your assignment.

Chris: Laura, my schedule's full.

Laura: It's your week.

Chris: I didn't receive my usual notification.

Laura: Yes, you did.

Chris: *(focused on computer)* I show nothing here on my schedule.

Laura: *(reaching into her briefcase)* Well, I show *here* on a copy of a memo sent to you, dated July 15, a reminder of the aforementioned assignment along with the breakdown of job descriptions and projected dates. As you can see, and I quote, "The week of August 26, Chris Timmons will take full responsibility for the upkeep and inventory of the household necessities." End quote. Any questions?

Chris: Not at this moment, Counselor.

Laura: I rest my case. Now what's on the schedule for today?

Chris: *(looking at computer)* Well, let's see. I've got a meeting—or make that *meetings*—from the time I leave here until 10:00 tonight.

Laura: Any possibility of a dinner meeting?

Chris: With you?

Laura: *(a bit frustrated by the question)* Yes.

Chris: Not tonight. *(looks at computer)* I've got an hour opening Wednesday, 3:00.

Laura: *(disappointed)* Nothing sooner? Tomorrow?

Chris: I'll be in L.A., remember?

Laura: Okay. *(discouraged)* Make it Wednesday; I'm open too. *(Writes it in her Day-timer.)*

Chris: All right. I'll put you in. Where we at?

Laura: "Johnny's?"

Chris: Takes me a half hour to get there. How about brown bagging it at my office?

Laura: *(not very excited about it)* I'll see you then.

Chris: Good. *(as he types it in)* Laura . . . brown bag . . . Wednesday. *(getting up, putting on suit coat)* Now, I've got to go. See you later.

Laura: I'll probably be asleep. I've got an early breakfast.

Chris: In the morning, then. *(starts to leave)*

Laura: *(decides to tell him now)* By the way, the results are in. *(Chris looks puzzled.)* It looks affirmative.

Chris: *(confused)* What?

Laura: *(another hint)* It's a go!

Chris: *(catching on)* Oh, all right. *(Sits back down, opens up computer, no emotion.)* What are we looking at then?

Laura: *(frustrated by his response or lack of it)* The projected date is February third.

Chris: February is bad . . . but I've got, what, nine months to rearrange my schedule.

Laura: *(not pleased, mocking him a bit)* There will also be some preliminary meetings that I'm told are necessary to have a full understanding of the project.

Chris: *(doesn't catch on)* Do you have those dates?

Laura: Not at this time. I'll get those to you ASAP.

Chris: I'd appreciate that. *(getting up to leave)* Well, congratulations. Job well done. *(grabs laptop)*

Laura: Thank you. Couldn't have done it without you.

Chris: My pleasure. Well, I'm late. *(turns to go)*

Laura: *(trying to get through to him)* Chris, we're having a baby. *(He turns back.)* We're having a baby!

Chris: Yes.

Laura: *We're*—you, me, we're together having a baby.

Chris: Yes. Well . . .

Laura: I can't believe it!

Chris: Well, I'm sure the doctor's office could send out a letter of confirmation.

Laura: Chris! I'm carrying your baby.

Chris: *(still not engaged emotionally)* Thank you for that vote of confidence.

Laura: Aren't you the least bit excited?

Chris: *(flatly)* Of course. Now, I have an appointment . . .

Laura: Will you forget about your stupid meeting. *(laughs with excitement)* Honey, we have a lot to talk about.

Chris: An hour on Wednesday.

Laura: An hour! First of all, I can't wait till Wednesday, and second of all, it's going to take a lot longer than an hour to prepare for this. There's the baby paraphernalia, morning sickness, maternity clothes, names.

Chris: I'm fully aware of that, Laura. It's just that right now I don't . . .

Laura: You drive me crazy, you know that.

Chris: Then I suggest you bring that up at our next scheduled performance evaluation.

Laura: Excuse me for a minute. *(goes to phone)*

Chris: Who are you calling?

Laura: The hospital.

Chris: Why? Is something wrong?

Laura: Yes. I'm going to see if they can give you a heart transplant.

Chris: Very funny.

Laura: He's got a sense of humor. All is not lost.

Chris: *(begins to leave)* You can reach me at the office.

Laura: *(angry)* No, I can't reach you at the office. I can't reach you on the phone. I can't reach you at home. I just got lucky one night and happened to reach you in bed. *(Chris, a bit stunned, just looks at her with a blank stare.)* What's happened to you? What's happened to us? We used to be alive, we used to be in love. Now, we're just . . . successful. I don't even know you any-more. Do I?

Chris: Laura, I appreciate what you're feeling here.

Laura: *(sarcastic)* Do you?

Chris: Yes. But now is just not the time to discuss it. I've got people waiting . . . *(begins to leave)*

Laura: Fine. Go.

Chris: *(stops, turns)* Like I said, we'll have—

Laura: An hour on Wednesday, I know.

Chris: Yes, and you'll have my un-divided attention. *(Laura says nothing. Chris feels somewhat bad.)* I'll see you tonight or in the . . . soon. *(He crosses to kiss her, but Laura only offers her cheek. He exits.)*

Laura: *(She stands there staring straight ahead. Slowly, very slowly, begins to break down, but then catches herself. Looks at her watch. Picks up phone, dials.)* Roger? Hi. Laura here. Lis-ten, about our client. What would you think if we flew out to actually show him the layout? I think if he was forced to look at it, he'd have no doubt. No, that's what I'd like to do. Tomor-row? *(looks in Daytimer)* I can't. Wednesday? *(pause)* Yes, that will work out fine. *(pause)* Just fine.

Lights slowly fade out.

Feeling Opposition

Phil and Kate visit their lawyer friend to draw up a will. Kate becomes very emotional as she envisions the will being needed (i.e., she or Phil dying). Phil, being "practical," tries to convince Kate she's overreacting (as usual). As they comically reach the point of actually signing the will, Phil gets a little surprise that releases an "overreaction" on his part . . . much to Kate's delight.

SUGGESTED TOPICS: thinkers versus feelers, marriage

CHARACTERS:

Phil	a "typically" unemotional male
Kate	a "typically" emotional female
Carl Stinson	a friendly lawyer

PROPS: Table, two chairs, papers, pen, box of Kleenex, envelope, tickets

Feeling Opposition

Donna Hinkle Lagerquist

Setting: *Lawyer's office. Couple going over some paperwork. The wife has been containing her emotions. The husband is quite laid back, but not cold.*

Stinson: Okay, everything looks good . . . all we need are a couple of signatures and it's legal.

Phil: *(cheerfully going to sign)* Okay . . .

Kate: *(grabs Phil's arm)* Ah, Mr. Stinson, could we have a few minutes alone?

Stinson: *(joking)* Sure thing. Phil, outa here, will ya? Your wife wants to see me alone.

Kate: No . . . I meant . . .

Phil: Carl, you nut! *(Both laugh, Kate doesn't. Stinson notices and then gets serious.)*

Stinson: *(to Kate)* Is there something wrong with the wording or . . . don't you understand?

Phil: No, it's fine, and I think we've used enough of your time, Carl. Kate—just sign it.

Kate: *(to Stinson)* Please . . . just a few minutes?

Stinson: Sure . . . I understand . . . the finality of the paperwork and all can be a little more difficult than anticipated . . . *(to Phil)* Happens all the time.

Phil: That's okay Carl, Kate'll sign it as is . . . C'mon Honey, he's a busy man, and we've been over all this many times!

Kate: *(to Stinson)* Please . . .

Stinson: Sure, I can give you a few more minutes. After all, Phil, you did see to it that our phone system got up and running the same day I moved into this new building . . .

Phil: Yeah, how's it working?

Stinson: Great . . . Well, there's a little glitch over at the reception desk, but . . .

Phil: Really? Let me take a look. *(Kate clears her throat. Phil gets the point.)* Hey, I'll send a repairman out first thing Monday, okay?

Stinson: Sure thing—and I'm still working on those Bulls tickets! *(exit)*

Phil: *(brief pause)* So, what's up?

Kate: How can you be so cold and unfeeling?

Phil: Are you talking to me?

Kate: Yes! Laughing, talking about glitches in the phones and basketball.

We're about to make a life-changing decision! *(starts to get teary-eyed)*

Phil: Kate, I think you are getting a little overemotional about this . . .

Kate: Overemotional? *(stifles a big cry)* We're talking about the future of our son!

Phil: Kate, really . . . *(smiling)*

Kate: *(emphatically)* I don't want Gerald and Mary to raise Tyler!

Phil: They won't.

Kate: *(points to paper)* They might! And they hardly know him!

Phil: Gerald and Mary are his aunt and uncle. It's logical that they—

Kate: They don't love him!

Phil: Yes, they do!

Kate: Not like we do . . . not like Jenny Kritchen does!

Phil: Jenny Kritchen . . . our baby-sitter?

Kate: Yes, she *loves* him!

Phil: *(chuckles)* Honey, we can't name a fourteen-year-old

Kate: baby-sitter legal guardian to our two-year-old son! That's crazy!

Kate: I get crazy just thinking of him sleeping anywhere but in his little race car bed . . . and anyone else putting little green Teenage Mutant Ninja Turtle Bandaids on his booboos, or someone else potty training him, or . . .

Phil: *(with a laugh)* No one else is gonna wanna do that! *(Kate glares at him. He turns serious.)* No one else is gonna do it. We're signing our will, not our death certificate!

Kate: Well, I feel like we are . . . I don't want to sign. I hate thinking about living without Tyler . . . or you . . . *(with tears, running and throwing her arms around him)* Oh, Phil, I love you so much!

Phil: I love you too, Kate . . . but why don't we go cuddle somewhere else besides Carl's office?

Kate: *(starts to be consoled then)* I never want to look at you lying in a casket.

Phil: *(lightly)* Oh, I'll try to be burned beyond recognition or something.

Kate: *(upset)* How can you say that?

Phil: I was trying to make you laugh.

Kate: I don't want to laugh. I'm sad.

Phil: If you laugh, you won't be sad.

Kate: But I am sad.

Phil: Well, you shouldn't be.

Kate: Stop telling me what I should or should not feel!

Phil: *(growing frustration)* Kate, we're only doing this because we're supposed to, it's wise, for you and me and Tyler . . . just in case. Everybody should have a will just like everyone should have car insurance . . . you just hope you never have to use it.

Kate: How comforting.

Phil: Kate, I'm so tired of you getting all emotional at the least little thing.

Kate: What? The possible future of our son is a little thing?

Phil: *(putting pen in her hand, walking her to the paper)* C'mon Kate, just sign it and I'll take you out for a late dinner and a little dancing.

Kate: I just want to go home.

Phil: No dinner? No dancing?

Kate: I want to go and hold my baby *(weepy)* and tell him I love him . . . don't you?

Phil: I'd rather hold you.

Kate: Uh! Have you no feelings at all?

Phil: Obviously none you're interested in . . . *(change of approach)* I guess I'm just being more practical about this.

Kate: "Mr. Practical." So what else is new! *(pause)* Would you cry if I died?

Phil: *(matter of fact)* I suppose. *(She looks.)* Yes, probably. *(another look)* Yes! Yes! I would definitely cry if you died. Look, Kate, I don't want to overextend my friendship with Carl. It's late, let's just sign this thing, and if we want to we can change it later.

Kate: *(pause, beginning to give in)* Promise?

Phil: *(excited by the progress he sees)* Promise . . . and I'm sure everything will look better tomorrow. *(hands her the pen again)*

Kate: *(lighter)* I hope so. I guess it's a good thing we're both not emotional wrecks. We'd never get anything done . . .

Phil: Yeah.

Kate: *(starting to sign)* Sometimes that practical side of you drives me nuts! *(Stops signing, brief pause, teary, throws herself on him again.)* But I'd really miss it if it wasn't around!

Phil: *(trying to extricate himself)* Okay, okay. *(guiding her hand to the paper)* Before you get going again . . . *(calls off)* Hey, Carl! We're ready!

Stinson: *(from offstage)* I'll be right there—just finishing up the paperwork!

Phil: *(after she signs)* Now, that wasn't so bad, was it?

Kate: *(not reacting)* Did he say he was finishing the paperwork? Do you think he's gonna charge us? I thought he was your friend!

Phil: Honey, he's a lawyer. He thrives on paperwork.

Kate: But we've been here over three hours . . . if he charges us the—

Phil: Kate, will you relax? Stay calm, get a grip!

Stinson: *(entering)* Okay . . . how did we do? *(looks at will)* Two signatures and a half a box of Kleenex left. Not bad!

Kate: I appreciate your giving us the extra time. I've never done anything like this before.

Stinson: No problem. I'll have Joyce put the finishing touches on it in the morning and drop it off Wednesday, okay?

Phil: Sounds great. Thanks, Carl.

Stinson: *(shaking hands with Kate and Phil)* Sure thing, Phil, Kate . . . I gotta run up to a client on the eighth floor . . . so if you could just close the door behind you?

Phil: Sure!

Stinson: Oh, here. *(hands envelope to Phil)* Good night! *(exits)*

(Shocked, Phil and Kate look at each other.)

Phil: I don't believe it! *(growing angry)* I install a new phone system for him and he pats me on the back and says, "Stop in with Kate anytime and we'll put together a will for you" . . . then he pats me on the back with a bill in his hand! *(hands Kate the envelope)* Of all the tricks!

Kate: Phil, maybe we—

Phil: *(mad)* How can someone be so cold and unfeeling . . . and sneaky too!

Kate: Maybe it's . . . *(begins to open the envelope)*

Phil: *(calling after him, very upset)* What's the matter, Carl, don't you even have a heart? Boy, did I have him pegged wrong. I have a good mind to rip out the whole system and . . .

Kate: *(holding up two tickets)* Take it to the Bulls game.

Phil: *(still mad)* How can you make jokes when . . . *(sees them, still shouting)* Were those in the envelope?

(She nods. Humbled, he lowers his voice.) No bill?

Kate: *(shaking her head)* You know, I get so tired of you getting emotional over the least little thing!

Blackout

IMPORTANT NOTICE: Purchase of this book entitles your church and/or nonprofit organization to unlimited use when used as part of your regular church services or nonprofit programs. This includes photocopying the scripts for each actor in *your church or organization only* and performance as often as you like at no additional cost or royalty fee. Use of the video or sketches for fund raising, television, radio, video, or commercial purposes is prohibited.

© 1992, Willow Creek Community Church

Tired When Needed

Mr. Watson has locked himself up in a motel room to get away from people and their demands on his time. However, Mrs. Willoughby has tracked him down to request his involvement in just one more worthy cause. He tries reason, and then a direct "no," but nothing works with Mrs. Willoughby, until he cracks.

SUGGESTED TOPICS: burnout, saying "no," boundaries

CHARACTERS:

Bruce Watson   a well-known, well-respected, and overworked member of his community

Mrs. Willoughby   an overbearing woman

PROPS: door with chain, bed, table, chair, nightstand, telephone, T.V. remote, suitcase, garment bag, junk food (popcorn, candy bars, Coke, 7-Up), rifle, blue jeans, vest, boots

Tired When Needed

Sharon Sherbondy

Scene: *Opens with Bruce entering a hotel room. He's carrying his garment bag and duffle bag. All appears normal. He sets his suitcase down, turns, and looks out the window.*

Bruce: Will you look at that view. *(mimes pulling curtains tightly together)* But this view. This takes my breath away. *(Crosses to shut the door, then locks it, making sure it's secure.)* Nice piece of workmanship here. *(Crosses to a table, opens duffle bag and dumps out junk food.)* This should keep me supplied for several days. *(Picks up a bag of popcorn and a candy bar.)* Let's see, salt or sugar?

(He decides on a candy bar, looks around, sighs deeply, and then jumps, landing flat on the bed. Grabs remote, turns on T.V. We hear "Gilligan's Island" theme. He sits up on his elbows, smiles, and begins singing along. Suddenly the phone rings. A look of panic comes over him. He turns off the T.V. The phone continues to ring. He jumps up and peeks out the window, checks the door once more, turns and stares at the phone. He slowly approaches the phone, picks it up.) Yes. *(pause)* Who's asking? Oh, my Mastercard? At the front desk. Yes,

well, thank you. Just hold it there for me and I'll pick it up next time I'm out. Thank you. *(hangs up)* Unless it expires first! *(takes a deep breath)* Boy, that was a close one. *(Turns the T.V. on again. He begins unpacking . . . blue jeans, a vest, boots. Then he unpacks a rifle, also in the garment bag. There's a knock at the door. He swings around, reflexively pointing the rifle at the door. He backs up, grabs the remote, and turns off the T.V. He sets the rifle on the floor by the bed, then looks around for a place to hide. Nothing looks good.)*

Mrs. W: *(from other side of door)* Mr. Watson. *(He's shocked that his name has been called.)* Mr. Watson. I know you're in there, Mr. Watson.

Bruce: I can't believe this!

Mrs. W: Mr. Watson. Please open the door. Mr. Watson. *(knocking continues)*

Bruce: *(reluctantly opens door just a crack, with the chain still on)* Mrs. Willoughby! What do you want?

Mrs. W: I want to talk to you.

Bruce: What about? How did you find me?

Mrs. W: *(speaking outside the door)* "Elementary, my dear Watson." *(He's not impressed with her attempt at humor.)* I simply called your wife who said you were out on business, then called your secretary who said you were unreachable, which we all know is quite false. I then put a tracer on your car phone which led me to this lovely, yet barren part of the state. I proceeded to stop at each gas station with a description of your car, which led me to this town, where I then called all the motels to find your registration. *(Watson slams the door in frustration.)* Oh come now, Mr. Watson. If you'd really wanted no one to find you, you would have hidden. Now may I please come in? *(Watson very reluctantly unlocks and unchains the door and throws it open for Mrs. Willoughby to enter.)* Well, my, what a cozy little room. Do you come here often?

Bruce: *(attempting courtesy)*
What is it you want, Mrs. Willoughby?

Mrs. W: *(sees the soft drinks and hints)* Besides something to drink?

Bruce: Coke or 7-Up?

Mrs. W: Oh, 7-Up would be lovely, thank you for asking. *(He gets it for her.)*

Bruce: *(she's already sitting)*
Would you like a seat?

Mrs. W: Why, thank you.

Bruce: Now, what is it you need, Mrs. Willoughby?

Mrs. W: Well, since you brought it up, we're having the annual fund drive In a few weeks, and I wanted to confirm the date and time for you to chair the kick-off meeting.

Bruce: Did I know about this?

Mrs. W: Oh, yes. We've corresponded with eight letters and five telephone calls.

Bruce: And what was my answer?

Mrs. W: Well, we never did hear directly from you, but knowing the kind of man that you are, dedicated to the people of our community, I never doubted you'd volunteer.

Bruce: Well, I'm sorry, Mrs. Willoughby for inconveniencing you like this . . .

Mrs. W: Oh, no trouble, no trouble at all.

Bruce: And for the delay in my response.

Mrs. W: I know you're a very busy man.

Bruce: But the answer is . . . no.

Mrs. W: What?

Bruce: I can't do it.

Mrs. W: Why?

Bruce: Because . . . because I'm tired.

Mrs. W: Tired of what?

Bruce: Tired of meetings, tired of committees, tired of . . . people.

Mrs. W: *(truly surprised)* Well, that's the most ridiculous thing I've ever heard.

Bruce: I'm sorry you feel that way.

Mrs. W: Sorry. What kind of joke is this?

Bruce: It's no joke, Mrs. Willoughby.

Mrs. W: I spend all day trying to track you down, not to mention the time and money spent on publicizing your involvement in this effort, and you have the gall to say you're tired.

Bruce: Mrs. Willoughby . . .

Mrs. W: This is for a very good cause, Mr. Watson. These are children, handicapped children, who are in desperate need of financial help.

Bruce: I know that.

Mrs. W: We need someone, like yourself, who can get the people involved. I mean, look what you've done for the hospital, the Lions Club, the community teen center, the church. *(giving it her best shot)* Mr. Watson, one can't get tired when one is needed.

Bruce: Mrs. Willoughby, there are other people . . .

Mrs. W: Mr. Watson, if I wanted someone else, I would be there, not here. I won't take no for an answer.

Bruce: Mrs. Willoughby, I'm sorry to disappoint you, but I just can't do it.

Mrs. W: Well, this just isn't like you.

Bruce: *(something triggers him off)* Like me?

Mrs. W: Yes, to turn your back on people.

Bruce: *(voice rising) Like me?*

Mrs. W: To play with people's emotions like this. You've always been so dedicated and sacrificing and . . .

Bruce: Mrs. Willoughby, what's my favorite color?

Mrs. W: What?

Bruce: My favorite food?

Mrs. W: Mr. Wat—

Bruce: My favorite author, T.V. show, hobby?

Mrs. W: How should I know?

Bruce: Red, lasagna, Ernest Hemingway, *Gunsmoke*, and *(grabs rifle, Mrs. Willoughby screams)* hunting!. *(He continues to talk with the rifle in his hand, quite agitated.)* So don't talk to me about what's like me and what's not like me when you don't know the first thing about me. *(pause)* I love our community, I love being a part of its growth and expansion. I love helping the kids, the people, raising money, dirtying my hands. But I need a break. Do you hear me? I can't do it anymore. *(Pause. Mrs. Willoughby is frozen in fear.)* I've spent my adult life campaigning for others but I'm losing . . . losing me along the way. So you see, how could you know what's like me or not like me, when *I* don't even know me. *(The rifle is now, inadvertently, in Mrs. Willoughby's face. He notices, then lowers the gun.)* Don't worry, Mrs. Willoughby, I'm not going to shoot you.

Mrs. W: *(starting to get up, careful not to turn her back to him)* You know, come to think of it, Dr. Leininger might be a good choice for the job.

Bruce: Yes, he is a good man.

Mrs. W: *(backs out of the door)* Well, I've taken enough of your time. *(slams the door)*

Bruce: *(said to shut door)* Good luck with the fund drive. *(He locks the door, then slowly goes to the bed, lies down. As he hits the T.V. remote, the lights black out.)*

I Don't Want to Fight You Anymore

This monologue is a conversation between a woman and God. She describes her frustration at obeying him and her struggles to be the new creation he desires. To her, God seems to demand a lot. She reminds God that she lacked a loving role model in her earthly father who controlled her, and now she isn't sure she's willing to let God control her life. But she's tired of fighting and needs to find relief.

SUGGESTED TOPICS: relationship with God, giving up control, our value to God

CHARACTERS:

one woman

PROPS: kitchen table, chair, coffee pot and cup

I Don't Want to Fight You Anymore

Debra Poling

Setting: *A woman sits alone at a kitchen table with a cup of coffee.*

Woman: Life was so much simpler before I met you. I woke up, ate breakfast, did whatever it was I was supposed to do that day, ate dinner, checked out the *Tonight Show*, and went to bed. I could justify anything. I mean I could sit in the Snuggery *(or insert the name of a local singles hang-out)* doing some networking late into the night. You know when in Rome . . . or I could "do a long lunch," without guilt, at the company's expense, or if someone cut me off on the tollway I could enlighten him with a few choice words. *(a bit sarcastic)* We all know it's not good to let anger build up! I was sailing through life just fine till you came along with your wave machine and knocked my little dinghy right out of the water. *(pause, sips some coffee, then says somewhat lightly)* Oh, it started out innocently enough—you wanted to save me from my sins and take me to heaven with you. Hey, I appreciate that. But now you want to interfere . . . *(catches herself)* get involved in my life, before I even get there. You say you've got some "guidelines" to live by. I can understand giving help to some poor soul who's at the end of his rope, but come on . . . You see my life . . . I have it ordered. I've got it all together—at least mostly together. So why complicate things by telling me I have to obey you? Have I done such an awful job on my own? Have I? *(pause, pours some more coffee)*

Besides, if you really understood me you would have never asked that . . . *(growing frustration)* Okay, you were there when I was growing up. You saw how hard it was to honor and obey my dad. I tried so hard to please him . . . did whatever I could to try to make him happy. I remember at first it was fun getting his slippers, or bringing him his coffee. I felt so grown up. I was Daddy's big

helper. Of course that's when I was good. When I was good, I was very good; when I was bad, I was horrid. Or so I was told. But as I got older I noticed it wasn't just, "Honey, would you please get your dad a cup of coffee?" but it turned into, "Honey, get me a cup of coffee . . . now! And why can't you do this better, and stop wearing all that makeup . . . makes you look cheap. Why aren't you more like Janet?" Needless to say, he had high expectations. Yeah, we were all Dad's little puppets. He was in control. *(pause)* And now *you* want control. It's like I can almost hear you say, "Come on, get me a cup of coffee . . . now."

(pause) You know, you scare me. You expect a lot. You want me to turn it all over . . . but I don't want to become someone's slave again. Surely you can understand that. I know. I know. You say you love me like no earthly father ever could. Well, I've got no earthly example of what

heavenly love is like. *(breaks down)* So I fight with you, to keep you at a safe distance . . . and I fight with myself because I don't want to give up control of who I am and what I want and what I do . . . and so I fight and I fight and I fight! *(long pause)*

Oh, God, I'm getting so tired of fighting. I'm so tired of fighting to control my life. Somehow I've got to get over this fear of you. Somehow I've got to see you . . . differently. Somehow I've got to see your hands reaching out to give to me and not take from me. *(very moved)* Somehow I've got to hear you say, "Honey, thanks for the cup of coffee. Come sit with me because you are a treasure."

(long pause) Life was so much simpler before I met you.

Slow fade to black.

Is "Nothing" Sacred?

Sam is invited by his friend Mark to a meeting of a new religious group that combines faith with science. As the meeting begins, Sam realizes this is a bizarre "religion." The "Nihilo Master" leads the members in the ritual, and he unveils the meaning behind all of life and the source of everything that is—a big zero. Everything has come from nothing, everything is going toward nothing, therefore everyone and everything is nothing. This is the message of modern scientific "religion," and this humorous satire leaves the audience laughingly aware of the logical outcome of such a worldview.

SUGGESTED TOPICS: evolution, creation, modern science

CHARACTERS:

Mark	member of the Star Brothers
Sam	Mark's friend
Nihilo Master	leader of the Star Brothers
Members of Star Brothers Group	at least four needed

PROPS: black robes, big "O" covered by a drape

Is "Nothing" Sacred?

Judson Poling

Setting: *Center stage is a draped object about four feet tall.*

Mark: *(entering, carrying two black robes)* Oh great, we're the first ones here tonight.

Sam: *(seeing no chairs)* Does everybody sit on the floor?

Mark: Actually, there are several different body postures we assume throughout the meeting. It's a very active religion.

Sam: You know, Mark, I have to say I'm really surprised that you're into all this.

Mark: Well, Sam, this group is a part of a whole new wave of truth seekers who are bringing together all branches of religious and scientific knowledge into a consistent metaphysic.

Sam: Still, you seem to be a pretty together guy to need a group like this.

Mark: Sam, when you find out the great truths of the universe, where we all came from and where we're all going, you can't help but be a together person. Listen, we need to put on our robes before the rest get here.

Sam: *(as he reluctantly puts it on)* You know, I feel silly doing this. Maybe I could just sit in the corner and watch.

Mark: Sam, you want to understand the cosmos, don't you? You have to be involved, not just watch.

Nihilo M: *(entering, followed by other Star Brothers, all with robes on, very eccentric)* Greetings, fellow Star Brothers. *(He holds his hands above his head in the shape of an "O" like a halo standing up on end, then bows).*

Mark: Greetings to you too, Nihilo Master. *(does the same)*

Nihilo M: I see we have a new Star Brother among us.

Mark: Yes, this is my friend Sam and he . . .

Nihilo M: *(shocked)* What did you say? Did you use a *personal* name just now?

Mark: Oh, I'm so sorry, Nihilo Master—it just slipped out.

Nihilo M: You know, Star Brother, that personality is an illusion—we are all one, and we must overcome using personal references even when it seems trivial.

Mark: Right. I just wasn't thinking.

Nihilo M: How else can we return to our Alpha Point unless we live consistently with our beliefs?

Mark: Yes, it won't happen again.

Nihilo M: *(abruptly changes subject)* All right, Star Persons, let us begin. *(They get into rows on two sides of draped object; Nihilo Master takes his position upstage center, also facing the object. Mark and Sam stand together with others.)*

Sam: *(as they are moving into place)* What did you call him before?

Mark: Nihilo Master.

Sam: Nihilo Master?

Mark: It's a Latin term.

Sam: Yeah, I know, but doesn't *nihilo* mean "nothing"?

Mark: Shhh! We're about to start.

Nihilo M: *(very affected)* All is one.

All: And one is all.

Nihilo M: As it was in the beginning—

All: Is now and ever shall be.

Nihilo M: *(grandiose)* We worship the source of our being, the ground of all that is, our Celestial Progenitor from which we came and to which we return. Let the symbol of that great fount of our creation be revealed to our unworthy mortal eyes. ZEE!

All: ROH! *(They move in a circle around object.*

Nihilo M: ZEE!

All: ROH! *(They chant the syllables slightly faster.)*

Nihilo M: ZEE!

All: ROH!

Nihilo M: ZEE!

All: ROH! *(circle gradually picking up speed)*

Nihilo M: ZEE!

All: ROH!

Nihilo M: ZEE!

All: *(very loudly)* ROH! *(Sam panics and screams amid the frenzy. The members return to original places around object.)*

Nihilo M: Let the unveiling proceed! *(They take off the drape. It is a zero, an "O" on a pedestal.)* Oh wonderful pri-

mordial soup of our substance, we worship you! *(Everybody goes to their knees, heads bowed, with hands above head in an "O.")*

Sam: *(still standing)* Hey! That's nothing! It's . . . it's a big zero!

Mark: *(looking up at him)* Have you no respect? You should be on your knees in reverence! *(Sam reluctantly drops to his knees.)*

Nihilo M: From nothing we came.

All: To nothing we return.

(Various Star Brothers call out.)

1: All pain and suffering, all of our problems, they are . . .

All: NO-THING.

2: All religion and myths about God are . . .

All: NO-THING.

3: The real meaning of life is—

All: NO-THING.

Nihilo M: What is everything that is?

All: NO-THING! *(All go completely down on floor and*

roll around making chaotic noises.)

Nihilo M: Yes, we are all merging with the equilibrium that is our primeval origin. Random-ness. Chaos. The great Alpha point, before it all began. *(This is too much for Sam. He begins to sneak out on his hands and knees; Mark grabs hold of his leg.)*

Mark: Where are you going, Sam?

Sam: Mark, I can't get into this!

Mark: Don't knock it until you've tried it.

(Sam pauses, decides to give it a whirl, and starts mimicking the others. He has some fun, not serious like the others.)

Nihilo M: *(As he talks, everyone is slowly rising to upright posi-tion; Sam continues his "an-tics" on the floor.)* And from this chaos we have finally evolved into our present form: slimy algae with arms, legs, and a backbone. *(Sam is now really into his "floor routine," a back-stroke accompanied by strange vocalizations. Oth-ers are all standing looking at him. All of a sudden he*

notices them. He's embar-rassed and stands to join them.) As it was in the be-ginning.

All: Is now and ever shall be.

Nihilo M: Everything from nothing and everything into noth-ing. Amen. The meeting is ended. *(All start talking.)*

2: Sushi and tea are out in the foyer for everybody! *(They all start to leave.)*

3: *(embracing Sam before exiting)* It's great to have a new Star Brother. *(Holds hands in an "O" above his head; Sam reluctantly cop-ies.)*

(Sam pulls the "O" down from above his head, looks at it—his hands.)

Sam: So, this is the shape of things to come?

Mark: Isn't it profound? Every time I come here, I learn some-thing new about myself.

Sam: You know, Mark, I'm learn-ing something new about you, too.

Mark: What's that supposed to mean?

Sam: How anybody can think we came from nothing and are going to nothing, so that now we're all basically nothing more than rear-ranged nothing . . . now, that's really something.

Mark: You're fighting it, Sam. You'll never reach your Omega point.

Sam: Sorry, Mark. *(he takes off robe)* This ain't my cup of tea. Whatever else I may *not* be, I *am* someone. Sorry if that doesn't qualify me as a Star Brother. *(as he exits)* Nanu, Nanu. *(like Mork from the "Mork and Mindy" television program)*

Blackout

Wonderfully Made

This sketch is an interpretation of the statement in Psalm 139 that God knits us together in our mother's womb and has a plan for our life. We see a child, Elizabeth, assigned qualities by God while in her mother's womb. She knows she is loved and made just the way God wants. However, once she is born, these feelings change because her parents' aspirations for her are quite different from what she was "told" in the womb. Their "redirection" through the years physically and emotionally stifles who Elizabeth was meant to be, and she grows up a sad and confused child.

SUGGESTED TOPICS: parenting, self-esteem, affirming uniqueness

CHARACTERS:

> **Female narrator**
> **God**   a male voice
> **Girl**   Elizabeth, a sensitive, introverted child
> **Father**
> **Mother**

PROPS: chair, coat tree, ballet slippers, large artist's paintbrush, soccer shoes, party hat, tickets, book, report card, canvas bag, running shoes, student council sign

Wonderfully Made

Donna Hinkle Lagerquist

Setting: *A simple chair center stage; behind it is a coat tree with the various props hung on it. Actors playing mother and father stand on either side of the coat tree, backs to the audience. A spotlight up on an actress kneeling frozen in a fetal position on the chair. She wears a black flaired skirt and black top.*

Female Narrator: *(heartbeat under)* God made all the delicate inner parts of her body and knit them together in her mother's womb. He made this child so wonderfully complex. His workmanship is marvelous . . . He was there when she was being formed in utter seclusion. *(heartbeat out)*

God: *(male voice)* This precious child, newly conceived, shall be a girl.

(Lights come up on entire stage area.)

Girl: *(comes to life, jumps up, and sings)* "I enjoy being a girl." *(curtsies)*

God: And you shall have the ability to dance and bring me delight in your movement.

Girl: *(sings and taps)* "On the good ship Lollipop, it's a nice trip to the candy shop . . ."

God: *(interrupts)* Well, that's good for starters. And you will be a painter.

Girl: Finger paints. Hurray! *(on hands and knees miming finger painting)*

God: To begin with, yes, but later watercolor landscapes that reflect my creation. *(Girl mimes creating a* *watercolor holding a palette, painting with her right hand.)* With your *left* hand.

Girl: *(switches hands)* Oops!

God: And you will delight in time spent *alone* in *creating* and *reading!*

Girl: *(disappointed)* Reading? An introvert? Aw, can't I be an extrovert . . . a real party animal!

God: *(forceful)* A precious *introvert!*

Girl: *(quickly)* Okay!

God: And, strong-willed!

Girl: *(with gusto)* Thanks!

Female Narrator: And God went on to create all the other specifics of this child—to make her precious and unique. And then he said to her . . .

God: My precious child, I love you. You are gifted and beautiful and made just the way I planned. I adore you, my child, and you will do great things! *(She listens intently and is visibly touched, hugs herself, sits and bends forward, grasping her knees, as though back in the womb.)*

Female Narrator: And this touched the child deeply, but then she was born. *(She slowly comes "alive.")* Because she was an introvert, she didn't make a loud and dramatic entrance. Time passed. She was a good child *(Girl puts on ballet slippers, which sit on the floor next to her chair)*, compliant and content to play by herself *(she picks up paintbrush, also on the floor, and stands up, dancing)*, despite her father's attempts to change her . . .

Father: *(turning around)* Elizabeth! Elizabeth! *(notices her)* Oh! Are you in here fooling around again? C'mon! We're going to soccer practice *(hands her two oversized soccer shoes which he has taken from the coat tree)*, and then to your cousin Randy's birthday party! What a great day, huh?

Girl: Well . . .

Father: Oh! And you can be my assistant when I do my magic show at the party. *(Plops a party hat on her head.)* How 'bout that, huh, huh?

Girl: You covered my ballerina hairdo!

Father: Hey, it doesn't matter what your hair looks like for soccer! Now hurry and get out of those silly ballet slippers! You'll be late for soccer . . . and I want you to make contact with the ball today! No cloud gazing! I'll be so proud of you! *(He goes back to his original position.)*

Female Narrator: So the child complied *(girl removes one slipper, puts on one shoe),* but only in part, for remember—she was also strong willed. And while deciding to put on just one soccer shoe, she had an idea.

Girl: I'll find Grandma at cousin Randy's party and snuggle up on her lap and pretend to be asleep when Daddy does his magic act!

Female Narrator: And she danced with delight at her great idea! Or at least she tried. *(Her movements are constricted by the soccer shoe.)* So she decided she better paint her idea *(kneels, picks up paint-brush, and mimes painting on paper on the floor)* in order not to forget it because she couldn't write very well yet . . . much to her mother's dismay.

Mother: *(turning around)* Elizabeth! Elizabeth! Are you drawing *again?* We're running out of room on our refrigerator. Are you wasting the lined paper I bought for you to practice your letters on? Well, since you are using it, make me an "E," the letter that your name begins with. *(Girl starts to write with her left hand.)* Don't use *that* hand! Your letters will look funny! I'll bet *that's* your problem. Your sister was writing at two and a half, and here you are almost five! Here, keep this hand behind your back. *(Mother puts girl's left hand behind her back.)* Now, make me a nice "E" or you can forget the ballet lessons! *(Girl struggles to make a shaky "E.")* You gotta do better than that! *(Goes back to her original position.)*

Female Narrator: And so the little girl felt confused, untalented, and unloved. She tried to comfort herself by dancing *(she tries, but now it is even more awkward with one hand behind her back and one soccor shoe on),* but it became almost impossible. And time passed.

Father: Elizabeth, Elizabeth! I have a surprise for you! *(He holds out tickets.)*

Girl: Tickets? *(excited)* Are they for the Nutcracker Ballet?

Father: *(annoyed)* The Nutcracker? You don't want to go to that. What a rip-off! The cheapest seats cost thirty bucks, and they're up so high you can't even see any of those dancers traipsing around on stage. These tickets are for the Auto Show. You can help Daddy pick out a new car! *(Father grabs her hand and pulls her along. She is very sad.)*

Female Narrator: And so again the child complied and followed along with her *parents'* plan. *(girl sits)* She danced less and less, her strong will faded *(she puts*

on the other soccer shoe), and she took up soccer and other sports to appease her father. *(She stands on a field during the soccer game as goalie and notices something on the ground. Her parents are now "cheering on the sideline.")*

Parents: Kick it! *(etc.)*

Girl: Oh! What a beautiful dandelion puff! *(She mimes picking it and blows on it. As she does a goal is scored.)*

Father: Elizabeth, stop the ball!

Mother: Elizabeth, pay attention!

Father: C'mon, you're the goalie!

Girl: *(sees imaginary ball go by)* Oops!

Parents: Elizabeth!

Female Narrator: And once again the child felt confused, untalented, and unloved. *(Girl goes back to the chair.)* She worked harder than most at school. Learning didn't come easily to her. She would much rather be painting *(She mimes* *putting down books and starts painting.)*

Mother: *(enters with a book and report card which she has gotten from a canvas bag hung on the coat tree)* Elizabeth, I see your report card here . . . Math—C, English—B, History—B, Spelling—C, Art—A+. What's with this C in spelling and math? If you worked as hard in these subjects as your painting, you'd get A's there too! *(shoving book under her arm)* You can't paint your way into college, you know! *(returns to original position)*

Father: *(enters)* Elizabeth, you need to get more involved in school activities. Like cross country *(puts shoes on her shoulder)* or student council *(puts a sign in her right hand—"Vote For Elizabeth!")*. It's not good for a girl your age to be so isolated! *(returns to original position)*

Female Narrator: *(as the girl stands weighed down with all her parents' "things")* And so the girl soon stopped painting and dancing altogether. She was very unhappy. And as she hung her head, she noticed her pink ballet slippers in one corner and her paintbrush in the other. Then, very faintly in the back of her mind, she remembers His words.

God: *(slow fade to original spotlight on girl)* My precious child, I love you. You are gifted and beautiful and made just the way I planned. I adore you, my child, and you will do great things!

The lights gradually fade out.

Other Willow Creek Resources Available

An Inside Look at the Willow Creek Seeker Service Video

An Inside Look at the Willow Creek Worship Service Video

One-on-One with Oliver North Video (an interview with Bill Hybels)

Sunday Morning Live Video, Volume 1

Sunday Morning Live, Volume 2

Sunday Morning Live Video, Volume 2

Walking With God Journal

Walking With God Series

> *Building Your Church*
> *Discovering the Church*
> *"Follow Me!"*
> *Friendship With God*
> *Impacting Your World*
> *The Incomparable Jesus*
> *Leader's Guide 1*
> *Leader's Guide 2*